Symbolism Reference Guide

And Dream Journal

By: Debbie Kitterman

Sound the Call Publications
A Division of Dare 2 Hear Ministry
PO BOX 5077
Lacey, WA 98509-5077

ISBN: 978-0-9840123-4-3

Scriptures with bolded portions are to express emphasis by the author.

Please take note that the name of satan and related names are not capitalized. The author chooses not to give him importance.

Cover photo by Johannes Plenio on Unsplash

Cover design and book layout by Brandi Kitterman, Create Media

Acknowledgments

To all my friends and family - Thank you for believing in me and encouraging me to pursue the dreams in my heart that I had long given up on.

Finally, thank you to Jesus Christ my Lord and Savior, it is because of you that all things are possible. Thank you for choosing an "ordinary nobody" to work through to make a difference in the lives of other people.

Dedication

I dedicate this book to my loving husband John and wonderful children Jesse, Brandi, and my daughter-in-love Jessica. Thank you for allowing me to follow my dreams and pursue the passion God has placed in my heart. You are all a treasure to me and a true gift from God.

Table of Contents

Welcome 9
    How to Use this Book 10
    Dreams 101..11
Part One: Basic Overview on Dreams 13
    Let's talk about Dreams...14
    Stay Focused...16
    Basic Understanding..17
    Types & Purpose of Dreams..19
    Symbolism...20
    Figuring it out 22
    Final Thoughts 25
Part Two: Symbolism Reference Guide 27
    Instructions 28
    Exercise 29
    Animals 31
    Buildings/Rooms...32
    Colors 33
    Exercise 35
    Directions 36
    Environment 37
    Exercise 38
    Forms of Communication...39
    Jobs/Trades...40
    Metal...41
    Exercise 42
    Modes of Transportation 43
    Numbers 44
    People/Family..45
    Places..46
    Water...47
    Miscellaneous..48
    A - Z Miscellaneous 49
Part Three: Dream Journal Pages...83
    Introduction 84
    Helpful Hints To Utilize This Journal 85
    Table of Contents...87
    Dream Journal and Interpretation Pages 92

Bible References to Dreams..142

Welcome

I am delighted you have picked up this newly revised symbolism reference guide and dream journal book.

This book is a combination of two previous best-selling Dare 2 Hear products. After fifteen years of utilizing these two separate books in classes and workshops, I have decided to refresh them and combine them together for ease of use. I want to give you tools that help you discern the messages God gives you in the form of dreams, pictures, and visions. Appendix 1 features an entire list of Scriptures related to dreams. You can also reference "Releasing God's Heart through Hearing His Voice" training manual to find many Biblical examples of how God used dreams in a variety of ways in both the Old and New Testament.

God speaks in order to deliver messages to His people. When He uses dreams, visions, and pictures, they are sometimes literal and sometimes allegorical. Literal dreams foretell events that will unfold just as in the dream. Allegorical dreams, visions, and pictures use symbols to convey meaning—these require interpretation.

In order to interpret dreams, visions, and pictures, we must understand the ways God uses symbolism. Throughout the New Testament, Jesus uses parables, word pictures, or stories that leverage symbols to convey meaning for the items used in the parables. The same is true each time we dream, have a vision, or God gives us a picture. He will use symbols that are specific just to us, or even specific to the person we are ministering to.

God will often use the same symbols in other dreams, visions, and pictures. He does this to develop a language with specific meaning to us. Over time, we begin to accumulate a list of symbols that God uses to speak specifically to us. Dreams, visions, and pictures are personalized by God to speak personally just to you! While books on dream symbols can help, we cannot use them alone as keys to unlocking our dreams, visions, or pictures. We must always ask ourselves, "What does this item or person mean specifically to me?"

The Bible is our foundation for everything, so we always look there before picking up a book or symbol reference book. Ask yourself, is this in the Bible? If so, then what is the reference and does the Bible have anything to say about this specific symbol? For example, symbols such as colors, numbers, certain animals, etc. are often found in the Bible. I will share more on this later.

How to Use this Book

There are three parts in this newly revised dream symbol and dream journal book:

Part One: Basic Overview of Dreams

This section outlines the basics of dreams and interpretation. It provides an overview on what dreams are, why they can be messages from God, and how to figure out what they mean.

Part Two: Symbolism Reference Guide

Part two covers symbolic meanings, give you some aids for discovering what symbols mean to you, and provides a place to record the specific meaning. The symbol journal is divided into sections. The more common symbol meanings are listed in the first section. If you find a symbol that has a meaning listed that is different than yours, then you should cross out what is listed and write in your personal label as the new meaning.

There is also space for you to add your own symbols in alphabetically order for ease of reference. If you are faithful to keep track of your personal symbol language, it will be easier for you to not only recognize the way God speaks to you, but to interpret what He is saying as well.

Part Three: Dream Journal Pages

Through my own personal experience and my experience helping others with their dreams, God inspired me to create a simple, easy way to record dreams, visions, pictures, as well as their interpretation. I have been known to write a dream down in a journal and then jot notes, thoughts, and interpretations on random pieces of paper or sticky notes, which is definitely not ideal. Often these "notes" would get lost or separated from the original dream thus I would lose the interpretation.

This journal serves as a resource for the present as well as a reference for easy retrieval of past dreams, visions, and pictures. Once you fill the pages of the dream journal portion, you can pick up any blank journal and continue recording your dreams, visions, and pictures using the format you will learn in this book.

The journal is designed in a way that makes it easy to locate a dream, vision, or picture as well as its interpretation all in one place when you want to refer to them Ultimately, this is your dream journal to use however you choose. At the beginning of section three, I outline a specific way I utilize my dream journal along with some helpful hints.

Dreams 101

Did you know it is a proven, scientific fact that everyone dreams?

Yes, it's true.

Scientists have proven that when our bodies enter into REM[1] sleep, we enter into a state where we dream. So, if we all dream, then why don't we remember all of those dreams?

There could be several reasons for this, but one reason could be a lack of understanding. By this, I simply mean that if you haven't received teaching on how God can use dreams to speak to His people you may not give them any attention. If this is the case, then a dream can easily become an unimportant piece of mental junk, or the strange food you ate the night before.

When I teach on dreams, there are always a few individuals who inform me that they do not dream, ever! However, since it is a proven scientific fact that all humans dream, I simply ask them to see what happens in the weeks after the teaching. I specifically pray over them and intentionally ask God to send dreams in the night and ask Him to speak specifically to them through dreams. It has never failed—I am soon overwhelmed with reports from amazed students that have "suddenly" started to dream.

Once they receive teaching on dreams and pray for God to speak to them, their spirit is awakened. Their natural mind is made aware that the average dream may be God speaking a message.

I grew up in a very conservative Christian denomination, and we didn't really talk about dreams, or that they could be from God. The first time I heard someone talk about dreams, I had two reactions. My first was a knee jerk reaction—this is insane; God doesn't speak to us through dreams. Shoot, God doesn't speak to us at all, or at least not to me. However, at the same time, my spirit leaped at the teaching on dreams. I was drawn to them, partly, because I am a vivid dreamer. I dream in color—bright, bold, technicolor dreams. So when someone said dreams could be a message from God, I had to know more.

Have you noticed dreams and visions are very prevalent in the world today? If you hadn't noticed, let me just say, dreams are indeed widespread today in large part due to the "New Age" movement. The enemy works overtime counterfeiting the authentic true things of God to confuse people. When people find out I teach on dreams, they immediately want to know more, and I am peppered with all kinds of questions. There are a number of Scriptures referring to visions and dreams throughout the Bible. But don't take my word for it, I encourage you to grab your Bible and a concordance and take a look for yourself.

In the Old Testament, generation after generation searched for the truth. In particular, Daniel lived in a time and society that didn't know the difference between the real truth and the perceived truth. Daniel, himself, was grouped with the astrologers, soothsayers, and magicians—the "New Agers" of his day. Ever since the Fall in the Garden of Eden, Satan has been trying to counterfeit the true things of God. In doing so, he has led many people astray. Society has always been given glimpses into the world's view of the supernatural perceived truth. We must be ready to respond to society's intrigue and give them the real truth.

> *"This is what was spoken by the prophet Joel: 'In the last days, God says, I will pour out my Spirit on all people. Your sons and daughters will prophesy, your young men will see visions, your old men will dream dreams. Even on my servants, both men and women, I will pour out my Spirit in those days, and they will prophesy.'"*
>
> (Acts 2:16 -18 NIV)

If you haven't received teaching on dreams and interpretation, then there is a list of resources I offer listed at the back of this book in the appendix. Or you can check out my website at www.debbiekitterman.com for a list of upcoming in person or online classes and workshops.

Part One:
Basic Overview on Dreams

Let's talk about Dreams

> *For God does speak in one way and even another way—yet no one may be able to perceive what He says. One kind of answer God give comes in the form of a dream—in a night-vision—When deep slumber comes to people who have lain down to sleep in their beds. Yes, this is often when He opens the ears of humanity, and seals their life-corrections in the terrors of the night.*
>
> (Job 33:14-16 The Voice)

According to Job 33, God does indeed give His people sealed instructions (NKJ), wisdom and instruction (TLB), warnings (NIV), and life-corrections in the form of dreams. These messages are often "sealed" in the form of parables, so we seldom recognize them as God speaking to us. If we never recognize that God is speaking to us, we can discount these messages or view them as "junk mail." But what if God is using these instructions to deliver answers to the questions, we have been petitioning heaven about?

It is my desire to give you a solid foundation pertaining to dreams, visions, and their interpretations. In order to build a solid foundation, there are five things we need to realize:

1. Be Aware

We need to be aware that the average dream can be God speaking to you. Yes, even those weird pizza dreams can be from God, so start paying attention to them.

2. Be Willing

If we're not willing to write/record our dreams, then we shouldn't expect God to give us one. Be ready and willing.

3. Be Prepared

Prepare for God to speak to you using the avenue of dreams by putting something to write with and on next to your bed.

4. Be Expectant

When you go to bed at night, pray and ask God to send you spiritual messages in your dreams while you sleep. Be excited and expectant, believing He will speak to you while you sleep.

5. Remember

God is Love and God is Supernatural—BOTH aspects and characteristics attract people. Individuals will be drawn to God because of the Supernatural and we Christians need to think of it as normal. Remember to be prepared to talk to believers and non-believers alike concerning their dreams and the potential messages from God because there was a time when you were not aware that God would use supernatural means to talk to you.

Dreams have been prevalent in our society for a while and a quick search online reveals dozens of articles and videos. I regularly run across people whose own experiences are largely influenced by the new age movement's views on dreams. However, we as Christians need to embrace and reclaim them as our own and understand that God can and does speak to people through dreams. He can speak to the believer, the unbeliever, and the pre-believer alike.

Scripture warns us that we have a real enemy set on leading us into deception, whispering lies to us, and is hellbent on destroying us. Satan has long sought to undermine God. He does this in subtle ways by imitating the things of God which can lead to doubt and unbelief. If we as believers do not discern the spirit[2] behind something we can be led astray and caught wandering down a path God never intended.

Many new age websites remind people that dreams are meant to unify the body, mind, and spirit which will provide insight into our true selves and give us a means of self-exploration. One particular website goes on to say that understanding your dreams will give you a better understanding of, and a way to discover your true self[3]. However, for the Christian, understanding and discovering our true identity and our true self comes from knowing God. It also comes from reading the Word of God, listening to Him, and lining our lives up with His Word. Apart from God, we will not fully understand who we are and whose we are. Yes, God can give us dreams that speak to our identity, our destiny, and His purpose for our life. But the powerful truth the new age, and our adversary Satan, wants to keep from us is that dreams are not the thing that unifies the body, mind, and spirit. God is! God is the one who brings unity and wholeness to us. He is the one who mends our broken and fragmented pieces. We are a three-part being made up of a body, a soul (mind), and a spirit. We are made in the image of God. He is our creator and He, God, is where we go to figure out who we are, and what our identity is. It is not dreams.

Be a God follower! We must follow His Word and what is written in it. Follow God the Father, the Son—Jesus, and the Holy Spirit 100%. DO NOT chase dreams but understand and accept that dreams are a part of the package and one of the ways God can speak to us. God speaks to people in a variety of ways and just one is the avenue of dreams.

Stay Focused

God speaks in a variety of ways; dream are just one way. We must always be careful to keep our eyes focused on the Giver of the visions and dreams, Jesus Christ, and not on the visions or dreams themselves.[4] Remember, God and the Bible are our source for everything; without Him we are nothing and we have nothing.

As we take a closer look into what Scripture has to say about dreams, I will also briefly cover visions because visions and dreams are very similar, with a few exceptions. Let's dive into some definitions as we begin to lay some groundwork.

Vision: Seeing images (either a picture or a series of pictures) unfold when you are **awake**.

The dictionary describes a vision as "the act or power of sensing with the eyes; sight; an experience in which a personage, thing, or event appears vividly or credibly to the mind, although not actually present, often under the influence of a divine or other agency."[5]

Dream: Seeing images (either a picture or a series of pictures) unfold while you are **asleep**.

The dictionary describes a dream as "a succession of images, thoughts, or emotions passing through the mind during sleep."[6]

The concept of both visions and dreams is that God speaks to an individual on the screen of their imagination, either while they are awake or asleep. Sometimes people will experience seeing images as they are waking up in the morning or just as they are going to sleep at night, and they won't know if they are dreaming or seeing visions. Honestly, it doesn't matter which it is; it is the message of what is being seen that is important.

Once an individual receives a vision or dream, the next step is to figure out what message, if any, God is trying to convey to the dreamer or vision receiver. One of the ways to figure out the message is to pray and ask God to reveal His message. Sometimes, God will give the message outright in the dream, meaning it is literal. We see a few instances of this in both the Old and New Testament. One example from the Old Testament is when God warns King Abimelech in a dream[7] to not sleep with Sarah because she is Abrahams wife and not his sister. Another instance of a dreams message being literal is when God gave Joseph several dreams[8] to protect a young Jesus Christ.

Another way to figure out a vision or dreams message is to apply God's symbolism language and ask for the Holy Spirit to impart the interpretation and the meaning. Again, Scripture is filled with examples of God speaking in symbols to convey His messages. We see symbolism when Jesus taught parables. He told spiritual truths in a way that had hidden messages so that those who would seek the truth would find them. He shared the deeper revelation with the disciples who followed him. The same is true when God gives dreams full of symbols. God can and does release hidden messages in dreams that are wrapped in symbolism.

Probably one of the most famous dream interpreters of the Bible is Joseph. Throughout Joseph's life we see him not only receiving dreams, but God giving him the ability to interpret them as well. Joseph interprets a dream while in jail[9] that involves needing God to reveal what certain objects and symbols represent. The same thing occurs several years later with the dream Pharaoh needs interpreted.[10] Joseph was not just a dream interpreter; he was also a dreamer. When we are first introduced to Joseph, it is because he has a dream[11] that he shared with his brothers and then his parents. Joseph's dreams were both literal and symbolic. It would be thirty years before the rest of the family would understand the full magnitude of a dream God gave Joseph. When Joseph shared dreams about wheat sheaves bowing down to him and even the dream with the sun, moon, and stars bowing to him, his father and brothers understood the message, but accused Joseph of being prideful and full of himself.

I hope by now you can see how very Scriptural dreams are. Not only are they Biblical, they are one of the many ways God speaks to His people. We need to be aware that the average dream could be God speaking to us. We need to be cautious about discounting it as a strange "food/ pizza" dream. Instead, we must seek God in prayer and ask Him if our dreams or visions are from Him and what they mean.

I want to help you better understand the steps to determine if a dream is from God and how to go about receiving its interpretation and message. So, here are a few things to understand:

Basic Understanding[12]

> *For God may speak in one way, or in another, yet man does not perceive it. In a dream, in a vision of the night, when deep sleep falls upon men, while slumbering on their beds, then He opens the ears of men, and seals their instruction.*
>
> (Job 33:14-16 NKJV)

1. Dreams and visions are similar to parables.

Scripture tells us God gives us sealed instructions in the form of dreams. These messages are sealed in the form of parables, so we might not recognize it is God speaking to us.[13]

2. The average dream can be God speaking.

Many people discount their dreams or view them as unimportant or "junk mail." When we do this, we often miss the real message just as many did in Jesus' time when He told parables. In actuality, dreams can be the answer to the very questions we have been asking heaven about.

3. People are drawn to dreams because of their supernatural revelation.

Christians need to think of dreams as being normal. Yes, they are natural, but also, they are a part of the supernatural. I like to say they are naturally supernatural. We need to view dreams as normal occurrences where God can speak a divine message to an individual. As Christ followers we also need to be prepared to talk to believers and non-believers alike about dreams.

4. God can speak to the non-believer through dreams.

God speaks to non-believers in hopes of bringing them to an understanding that He is real and to turn their hearts toward Him. In Scripture we see God speaking to the following individuals who did not believe in or follow Him: King Abimelech,[14] Laban,[15] Pharoah's butler and baker,[16] Pharaoh,[17] Midian,[18] King Nebuchadnezzar,[19] the wise men,[20] and Pilate's wife.[21]

5. Not all dreams are from God.

Dreams can have three sources: God, self, or the enemy. Any time we receive a dream, we must seek God and ask Him to help us discern the source.

6. Dreams are Biblical and Scriptural.

Just because the enemy has counterfeited the realm of dreams and dream interpretation, it doesn't mean we need to reject them, too. To reject the supernatural realm of dreams would not be Scriptural. Daniel[22] was a man who interpreted dreams. During his time, the world didn't understand the difference between the source of Daniel's knowledge and understanding and the other wise men serving the king. Daniel served God in humility and obedience and, in return, God allowed Daniel to excel in the area of dream interpretation. God's favor on Daniel allowed him to be in charge of all the wise men.

7. Be willing to record and write out dreams.

Scripture tells us that dreams fly away,[23] so we need to be willing to write out and record our dreams, visions, and pictures which we believe are from God. We do this so we can capture the details while they are fresh in our minds. Writing out our supernatural encounters with God, such as dreams, visions, and pictures, helps us when we later go back and reference the details in order to interpret, remember, and review them.

Types & Purpose of Dreams[24]

God uses dreams in a variety of ways. From Scripture and my personal experience, here are some of the types, ways, and reasons God can and does give dreams to individuals:

Protection/Warning

Protection/Warning dreams reveal impending danger or pitfalls the enemy has set up for us. They can warn us of things in our life that are out of control and may need to be dealt with. These types of dreams can be given to either the person who is in harm's way or to the person intending to do the harm.

Inquiring of your heart

Scripture tells us that God looks at the hearts of individual to reveal what is really there.

Prophetic

Prophetic dreams reveal God's plans for the future. The events of these dreams may not occur right away, but rather speak of the prophetic destiny God has for the dreamer.

Promotion and Favor

Scripture shows two kinds of promotion and favor dreams. One is where an individual will get a physical position or job promotion. The second is God placing His favor on people allowing doors of promotion and favor to open to them.

Instruction and Guidance

God gives dreams to His people to guide and direct them on the paths He wants them to take.[25]

Understanding and Teaching

God will often give instruction to His people to aid them in making decisions and right choices.

Confirmation

God can give us confirmation dreams that provides assurance that we are headed in the right direction. These types of dreams can also give us the courage to stand our ground and conquer our fears.

Strategy

God can give both life and business strategies to solve problems and lead to our success.

Plus More[26]

Symbolism

From the beginning of time, people have made symbols a part of their language. Today, we have universal signs and symbols such as traffic lights, stop signs, hands raised in surrender, and even a finger lifted to the lips to quiet or hush someone just to name a few. No matter where you are, when you see a universal symbol, you can easily have an understanding of what is happening around you. We see God using symbolism throughout the Bible. Jesus used parables to obscure some messages so that only those disciples who were with him could understand.

Throughout the Gospels we see Jesus telling parable after parable.

In Matthew 13:10 NIV the disciples finally ask, "Why do you speak to the people in parables?"

Jesus' response was in verse 11:

> *"The knowledge of the secrets of the kingdom of heaven has been given to you, but not to them."*

And He again responds in verses 13-16:

> *"This is why I speak to them in parables: Though seeing, they do not see; though hearing, they do not hear or understand. In them is*

fulfilled the prophecy of Isaiah: 'You will be ever hearing but never understanding; you will be ever seeing but never perceiving.'"

As Jesus was telling parables, He was revealing the secrets to the kingdom, and when the disciples didn't quite get it, they simply asked Jesus to share what He meant. The parables Jesus told were simply word pictures … stories the people living in those days and times could relate to.

In Matthew 13, Jesus tells the parable of the sower and the seed. The people Jesus spoke to were farmers; that is how they made a living and provided for their families. His audience easily understood and drew parallels between what Jesus was saying and their own real-life experiences. Yet, there was, and is, a deeper spiritual message in Jesus' parables that was overlooked by both Jesus' original audience and sometimes by contemporary readers of the Word today.

Some messages God sends us require interpretation. In order to interpret dreams, visions, and pictures, we must realize God often uses symbolism. Each time you dream, have a vision, or God gives you a picture, He can use symbols that are specific just to you. When God does this, He is creating language of symbols with you, and He will often use the same symbols in other dreams, visions, and pictures. Over time, you will begin to accumulate a list of symbols God uses to speak to you.

Just like parables had hidden spiritual messages in Jesus's times, the same is true for us. Dreams, visions, and some pictures are personalized and designed by God to speak to you! Because of this intimate, specific language of symbols God wants to develop with you, it's important to remember something: While books on dream symbols can help you, you cannot use them as the only key to interpret your specific dreams, visions, or pictures.

The dictionary states symbolism is "the practice of representing things by symbols, or of investing things with a symbolic meaning or character; the use of any of certain special figures or marks of identification to signify a religious message; symbolic meaning or character."[27]

I will give more specific examples of this later in the Symbolism Reference Guide. But for now, let me share this example: if my husband and I both had dreams about a dog, our meanings for the "dog" symbol would be completely different. I enjoy and love dogs; he, on the other hand, does not. If I tried to interpret my dream with his meaning for a dog, I would not have a true representation of what the dream could mean. If either one of us was indifferent to dogs, then we would look to Scripture. There we'd discover dogs often represented things that were dirty, unclean, or demonic.

Once God speaks to you using a certain symbol and you label it; He will often continue to speak to you using the same symbol to mean the same thing. For example, in my own life, when God shows me a picture of a bow and/or an arrow, I know He is showing me something about prayer, intercession, and spiritual attacks. This might not make sense to you, but it does to me.

The first time I received a picture of a bow and arrow, I was praying over a person, and the Lord showed me she was a powerful intercessory warrior. He went on to reveal that her prayers were creating barriers around individuals she would pray for so the fiery darts of the enemy couldn't harm them. Sometimes in the spirit realm, I see arrows flying at people and I know to ask them if they have been under spiritual attack.

My suggestion is that you keep track symbols God uses with you and what they specifically mean to you. That is why I created the Symbolisms Reference Guide. I needed one place to keep track of the symbols as I labeled them. If you are faithful to keep track of your personal symbol language, it will be easier for you to recognize the way God speaks to you. This is a vital step in growing in your ability to hear from God and in interpreting the messages He imparts to you.

If we are unable to label a symbol or have no point of reference as to the symbol's meaning, then the Bible should always be the first source to which we turn for determining the symbol's meaning. Scripture is full of symbolic meanings for things such as colors, numbers, and animals. Scripture lists several symbolic references for Jesus, the Holy Spirit, believers, and even Satan.

When people show up in our dreams, be cautious of assuming the dream is a prediction of events that will happen to the person. More often it's more important to understand what a person represents to you. Just as there are a list of questions to help you figure out what a specific symbol represents, there are questions you will need to ask to aid in figuring out what a specific individual may represent in your dream and your life. Not to worry, though, understand God is speaking to you specifically, and He wants you to understand the message, too.

Figuring it out

The Bible is full of dreams that God gave to individuals, both in the Old Testament and New Testament, for a variety of reasons. I firmly believe if He did it then, He will do it now, and He will continue to do so in the future.

Why do I believe this to be true? Because the Bible tells me so:

Jesus Christ is the same yesterday, today, and forever.
(Hebrews 13:8 NKJV)

Whenever God speaks to us, it will always line up with the Word of God.

In order to figure out what things mean to you, there is a list of questions you should ask yourself. You will find this list of questions in Part Two: Symbolism Reference Guide.

Interpretation

Dream interpretation is like solving a good brainteaser. You have to be a good sleuth, dig for clues, discover hidden meanings, and have patience. The thing that will help you the most is to ask question after question. Come at it from every angle and pray as you go through the process that God will reveal to you His specific message.

Remember, Scripture tells us interpretation belongs only to God. Both Joseph and Daniel understood that man cannot unlock the mysteries God speaks in dreams unless God gives the key. Most interpretation begins in the natural and ends in the supernatural when God reveals something.

> *"We both had dreams," they answered, "but there is no one to inter-pret them." Then Joseph said to them, "Do not interpretations belong to God? Tell me your dreams."*
> (Genesis 40:8 NIV)

> *Daniel replied, "No wise man, enchanter, magician or diviner can explain to the king the mystery he has asked about, but there is a God in heaven who reveals mysteries."*
> (Daniel 2:27-28a NIV)

So, how do you pull all this information together to figure out what message God is speaking to you? Again, we look to the Bible.

There are examples of God-given dreams and the interpretations throughout the Scripture. A favorite one of mine to point people to is in Genesis 41. In this chapter, we see God speaking to Pharaoh who, by the way, is a non-believer. Pharaoh is not given one dream—he is given two dreams! In Genesis 41:7b-8 (NIV) it says:

> *Then Pharaoh woke up; it had been a dream. In the morning his mind was troubled, so he sent for all the magicians and wise men of Egypt.*

Pharaoh told them his dreams, but no one could interpret them for him.

Drum-roll, please—enter Joseph, finally out of prison, because the cup-bearer "suddenly" remembered Joseph interpreted a dream for him that was exactly right on. Pharaoh asked Joseph to interpret his dreams, but Joseph responded with:

> *"I cannot do it," Joseph replied to Pharaoh, "but God will give Pharaoh the answer he desires."*
>
> (Genesis 41:16 NIV)

Joseph makes sure that everyone knows God is the one who is interpreting the dream, and that Joseph is just the vessel through whom God is speaking. We must also remember the same thing: Interpretation belongs to God! When God speaks, He wants His people to understand the message. He can use other people to interpret dreams, but God is the one who is speaking to them. This Biblical dream example is a lot like the parables Jesus shared in the New Testament.

How so, you ask?

As Jesus shared parables, He talked about things people understood, like planting, harvesting, yeast, etc. When we look at Pharaoh's dream in Genesis, there are things the people would understand, like the significance of the Nile River, which was the life flow in Egypt. They would also have understood heads of grain, cows, and the number seven. However, God told Joseph the significance of the two sets of seven cow and heads of grain.

As we continue to read Genesis 41, Joseph goes on to not just interpret, but label, the important key pieces in the dream.

> *Joseph said to Pharaoh, "Pharaoh's two dreams both mean the same thing. God is telling Pharaoh what he is going to do. The seven healthy cows are seven years and the seven healthy ears of grain are seven years—they're the same dream. The seven sick and ugly cows that followed them up are seven years and the seven scrawny ears of grain dried out by the east wind are the same—seven years of famine.*
> *"The meaning is what I said earlier: God is letting Pharaoh in on what he is going to do. Seven years of plenty are on their way throughout Egypt. But on their heels will come seven years of famine, leaving no trace of the Egyptian plenty. As the country is emptied by famine, there won't be even a scrap left of the previous plenty—the famine will be total. The fact that Pharaoh dreamed the same dream twice empha-*

sizes God's determination to do this and do it soon."
(Genesis 41:25-32 MSG)

Once you receive a dream, write it out, and label the symbols; the last piece is figuring out the interpretation. The interpretation comes through prayer and Holy Spirit revelation. We label all the pieces in the dream and allow God to breathe on them.

Final Thoughts

God is a loving Father and a loving father communicates with His Children. As children of God we need to know and understand that He wants to speak to us. The word of God is full of the many ways God has spoken in the past. Dreams are but one avenue for His communication. We need to recognize and accept that He may choose to speak to us through the avenue of dreams.

If God gives you a dream, it means He wants to open up the lines of communication. My strong suggestion for you is to NOT try to interpret other people's dreams. Being able to interpret other people's dreams is a gift from God and requires carefully listening to the Holy Spirit. God does indeed anoint some in dream interpretation, but I strongly believe that if God gives you a dream, He wants to give you the interpretation as well. I do, however, want to encourage you to talk to respected, Godly people with whom you are in an open, honest relationship. Prayerfully talk through your dreams, labels, and interpretations with them. Talking it out and getting feedback and suggestions from others can helps us see things we may have missed or not thought of before. God wants to develop your spiritual muscles in the area of dream interpretation. There are those whom God has given the gift of dream interpretation, but it is always the dreamer's responsibility to pray over and get their own confirmation of what God could be saying.

Part Two:
Symbolism Reference Guide

Instructions

To use the *Symbolism Reference Guide* section, you will need to *"figure out"* what specific symbols mean to you.

On the next few pages there are activation exercises. These exercises are designed to help you "figure out" what specific items can mean to you. I have included some common thoughts on what certain symbols can represent. Review the list and circle the one you identify with the most.

If you are unable to figure something out, remember to look to the Bible before utilizing a dream symbol book. You can do this by using a Bible Concordance or Bible Dictionary to help you locate passages of Scriptures that use the particular word you are investigating.

It is also important to note that when we dream about individual people in our dreams, it is not necessarily the individual, but what they represent. Below is a list of questions to ask about a person or a group of people in your dreams:

- What does this person mean to me?
- How are they connected to me?
- What are the qualities (good or bad) that come to mind with this person?
- What are the character traits of this person?
- What is the person's relationship to me?
- Neighbor, boss, father, mother, brother, etc.
- What are some descriptive words (adjectives) that come to mind about this person?

Throughout the book, you will find more pages and exercises designed to help you understand what a particular person, place, or thing represents to you.

Exercise

Let's walk through the process you will go through to figure out what a symbol can represent to you. If you have a dream, vision, or a picture with a dog in it, you will need to figure out what it represents to you. In order to do this, I suggest you ask questions. Below are sample questions:

- What does a dog mean to me?
- What are some things that come to mind when I see a dog?
- Notice if it is a particular breed of dog.
- What is that breed known for?
- What are common phrases people use when referring to a dog?
- I have started a list below for you on what a dog could mean.
- Look over this list and if something comes to your mind that isn't listed, write it in the spaces provided.

Dog
- Loyal companion/Loyalty
- Man's best friend
- Pet habits
- Special Things
- Excitement
- Protection
- Puppy love
- Misplaced Affection
- Unexpected Attack – if a child or someone you know was
- Attacked by a dog
- In the Bible: Dogs often represented things that were:
- Dirty
- Unclean
- Demonic
- _____
- _____
- _____

Once you have listed some of the things a dog could represent, you need to figure out what it could symbolize to you.

Step One: Read back over the entire list and pay attention to the ones you are most drawn to.

Step Two: Circle the one that has the most significant meaning to you. This would be what a dog would represent to you.

Step Three: Turn to page 31 under the heading titled "Animals."

Step Four: Now write your meaning for what a dog represents to you.

Let's work through another example.

For this exercise, we are going to figure out what a book can represent to you. Here are a few of the questions you may want to ask:

- When you think of a book what comes to mind?
- What could a book symbolize to you?
- What kind of book was it?
- Was it the Bible?
- Was it a child's story book?
- A fiction book?
- A Reference book?
- A Biographical book?
- An Autobiography?

Book
- Learning
- Entertainment
- Information
- Knowledge
- Education

- _____
- _____
- _____

Step One: Read back over the entire list and pay attention to the ones you are most drawn to.

Step Two: Circle the one that has the most significant meaning to you. This would be what you would then label a book.

Step Three: Turn to page 50 in the Miscellaneous section, under the heading of the "B's."

Step Four: Now write the meaning for what a book represents to you.

Animals

Ant...................................Hard working, industrious, stinging
Bear................................Danger, destruction
Beaver............................Industrious
Bees...............................Stinging words, gossip
Donkey...........................Stubbornness
Eagle..............................Leader, seeing from God's perspective
Horse..............................Man's plans and ways of doing things, authority, strong
Monkey..........................mischief, foolishness
Wolves............................Deceit
Dog.................................
Dragon Fly......................
Ostrich............................

_____

_____

_____

_____

_____

_____

_____

_____

_____

_____

_____

_____

_____

Buildings/Rooms

Your house .... Your life
Kitchen .... What you are feeding on, preparation, teaching
Bathroom .... Cleansing, purging
Bedroom .... Rest, intimacy
Living Room .... Your life at that moment
Upstairs .... Your mind, thought life
Basement .... Old stored issues, fears, hurts, etc.
Attic .... Mind, thinking, old thoughts, storage
Front Window .... Future
Back Window .... Past
Window .... Vision
Front Porch .... Prophetic vision

_____

_____

_____

_____

_____

_____

_____

_____

_____

_____

_____

_____

_____

Colors

White...............................(+) Purity, holiness, righteousness
　　　　　　　　　　　　(-) Blank, lacking zest

Green.............................(+) Life, growth, prosperity, conscience
　　　　　　　　　　　　(-) Envy, jealousy, pride

Black ....(+) Mysteries of God
　　　　　　　　　　　　(-) Sin, darkness, mourning, evil, calamity

Red ....(+) Passover, blood atonement (Jesus' Sacrifice),
　　　　　　　　　　　　wisdom, anointing, power, protection
　　　　　　　　　　　　(-) Anger, war

Blue ....(+) Presence of God, Holy Spirit, revelation,
　　　　　　　　　　　　communion, heavenly
　　　　　　　　　　　　(-) Depression, sorrow, anxiety

Purple ....(+) Royalty, authority, kingship, majesty
　　　　　　　　　　　　(-) False authority, self indulgence, extravagance

Gray...............................(+) Wisdom (hair color)
　　　　　　　　　　　　(-) Compromise, weak, old, wishy-washy

Pink ....(+) Feminine
　　　　　　　　　　　　(-) Flesh

Orange............................(+) Holy Spirit Baptism, praise, perseverance, purify, refine, con-
　　　　　　　　　　　　suming fire, refine, worship
　　　　　　　　　　　　(-) Caution, stubbornness, strong-willed

Brown.............................(+) Compassion, humility, "root" of an issue
　　　　　　　　　　　　(-) Flesh, humanity, humanism

Yelow ....(+) God's glory, gift of God, hope
　　　　　　　　　　　　(-) Timidity, fear

Gold...................................(+) Godhead, divine nature, holy, purity, glory
                                     (-) Idolatry
Silver..............................(+) Word of God, redemption
                                     (-) Legalism, slavery, domination

Rainbow ....God's Promises

_____

_____

_____

_____

_____

_____

_____

_____

_____

_____

_____

_____

_____

_____

Exercise

Dragon Fly
- Ornamental
- Colorful
- Contrast: beautiful – but the name is harsh – Dragon.
- Appealing, underlying meaning
- Vicious, undermining, kill their own
- Fast/Speed
- Annoying
- Beautiful simplicity
- _____
- _____
- _____
- _____

Now turn to page 31 and record your symbol for a dragon fly.

Ostrich
- Head in the sand
- Deceptive: appearance is deceiving – it doesn't fly
- Speed – fast runner
- _____
- _____
- _____
- _____

Now turn to page 31 and record your symbol for an ostrich.

Directions

South ....Away from God
East................................Settled
West...............................New frontier
North ....Going toward God
Left................................Closest to your heart
Right..............................Authority, God's right arm extended with Power

_____

_____

_____

_____

_____

_____

_____

_____

_____

_____

_____

_____

_____

_____

_____

_____

Environment

Morning.............................New day
Noon.................................At the peak of brightness
Night ....Unable to see apart from light of God
Dry ....Spiritually dry
Rain ....Anointing (If you wear glasses, could mean distorted vision.)
Desert ....Place of temptation, testing, refining
Mountain ....High experience, obstacle
Spring..............................New beginning, new growth, refreshing
Fall ....Harvest, change of season
Winter..............................Hibernation, dormant
Summer ....Fun, vacation
Clouds ....
Thunder Clouds...............

_____

_____

_____

_____

_____

_____

_____

_____

_____

_____

_____

_____

Exercise

Clouds can have different meanings depending on the type of cloud(s) you see. Let's use the following example for a regular
cloud.

Clouds
- If raining, bringing darkness or cover if light and airy
- Cover
- Perfection
- Daydream
- Bringing rain (anointing)
- _____
- _____
- _____
- _____

Now turn to page 37 and record your symbol for clouds. Now take it one step further. What if you saw Thunder Clouds? What would they mean to you?
- _____
- _____

Calendar
- Time
- Date
- Appointment
- Event
- _____
- _____
- _____
- _____

Now turn to page 51 and record your symbol for calendar.

Forms of Communication

A letter............................Communication, Word
Telephone.......................Communication, hearing
Email ....Communication from God's Word
Doorbell ....God is at your door
Knocking on door ....God is knocking on your door
Radio ....Tune in

_____

_____

_____

_____

_____

_____

_____

_____

_____

_____

_____

_____

_____

_____

_____

Jobs/Trades

Banker .... Finances
Teacher .... Training, educator
Professor .... Higher learning, educator
Lawyer .... Advocate
Judge .... Authority, dispensing judgement
Doctor .... Healer, physician

_____

_____

_____

_____

_____

_____

_____

_____

_____

_____

_____

_____

_____

_____

_____

_____

_____

_____

Metals

Gold................................Purity, glory
Silver..............................Refining
Steel...............................Strong, tested in the fire
Titanium..........................Strong

_____

_____

_____

_____

_____

_____

_____

_____

_____

_____

_____

_____

_____

_____

_____

_____

_____

_____

Exercise

Train

- Can run you over and leave devastation in its path
- Historic – 19th century
- Powerful move of God – right on track
- Moving forward
- Well-laid plans
- Continuous work
- Transport cargo
- Travel
- Innovation
- Ministry
- _____
- _____
- _____
- _____

Now turn to page 43 and record your symbol for a train.

Modes of Transportation

Car..Your life or ministry in motion.
Note: It is important to pay attention to who is driving your car and what they may represent to you.

A convertible..........................(+)Free in the Spirit, adventure
(-)uncovered

A sports car ....Fun, adventure

Van or bus ....Doing something that involves others

Driving from the back seat...You are not in charge

Your car parked.....................Your life or ministry is on hold

Flat tire on your car..............Losing spiritual life

Bicycle ....Doing it your own efforts

Motorcycle ....Doing it in God's ability but alone

Airplane.................................Getting into the spirit realm

Helicopters ....Angels

Roads......................................

    Shady................................Prayer

    Muddy ....Getting stuck

    Dusty ....Spiritually dry

    Four-lane highway...........In the flow

    A lot of traffic ....A lot of traffic- too busy

Train ....

_____

_____

_____

_____

_____

_____

_____

_____

Numbers

1 ....Beginning, Unity, God
2 ....Divide, # of division, multiplication, confirmation, witness
3 ....Unity, Godhead, confirmation
4 ....Preparation - time of testing, world
5 ....Grace, wisdom, supernatural aspects of God, redemption, anointing
6 ....Man
7 ....Perfection, completeness, fullness, fulfillment, rest
8 ....New Birth, new beginning, Teacher*
9 ....Manifestations of the Holy Spirit, gifts/fruits of the Spirit, harvest, judgement, **Evangelist***
10 ....Set apart unto the Lord, Ten Commandments, test and trials, journey, wilderness, nurture, Pastor*
11 ....Prophetic, transition, standing in the gap, Prophet*
12 ....Set apart to God's purposes, divine government, Apostle*
13 ....Rebellion, double portion (Gen 14:4)
14 ....Double anointing, bridal love, deliverance (Gen 29:29-30)
15 ....Rest, reprieve, mercy
50 ....Jubilee

_____

_____

_____

_____

_____

_____

_____

_____

_____

_____

* The 5 fold offices referred to in Ephesians 4:11

People/Family

Questions to ask about a person or a group of people in your dreams:
- What does this person mean to me?
- How are they connected to me?
- What are the qualities (good or bad) that come to mind
- with this person?
- What are the character traits of this person?
- What is the person's relationship to me? Neighbor, boss,
- father, mother, brother, etc.
- What are some descriptive words (adjectives) that come to
- mind about this person?

Father .... God
Mother .... Holy Spirit
Brothers and/or sisters .... Body of Christ
Grandmother .... Special tender side of Holy Spirit
Best Friend .... Jesus
Best friends .... Support, nurture, encouragement
A child .... Child-like faith, innocence, someone's ministry
Your child .... Your ministry or responsibility
An old friend from the past ... An old habit

_____

_____

_____

_____

_____

_____

_____

_____

_____

Places

School .... Training
Bank .... Finances
Hospital .... Spiritual healing/surgery
Hotel............................... Travel, temporary

_____

_____

_____

_____

_____

_____

_____

_____

_____

_____

_____

_____

_____

_____

_____

_____

_____

_____

Water

Water ....The Holy Spirit, the anointing
Ocean ....The vastness of God or God's plans, also humanity as a whole
Flowing water ....Flowing in the anointing
A river ....A large move of God
A pond............................A local church
Stagnant water.................No flow of the Holy Spirit
Dirty water ....Mixing sin or flesh with the Holy Spirit
Rain...............................Outpouring of God's anointing

_____

_____

_____

_____

_____

_____

_____

_____

_____

_____

_____

_____

_____

_____

Miscellaneous

Lost your glasses................ Not seeing clearly
Huntin .... Searching for God
Pregnant .... A new ministry or responsibility
                                  Hint: Pay attention to what stage of pregnancy.
Your Mother's house.......... Bull's eye, right in the center of God's will
Going to your mother's house... Headed toward the center of God's will
Your old home where you
were raised .... Roots
Going to the bathroom in a
public area........................ Need to publicly apologize or need to handle something openly.
Gray hair .... Wisdom, age
Toys.................................. Gifts or distractions
Purse................................ Identity
Wallet .... Finances
Keys .... Access, authority, entrance, permission to enter
Antiques .... Inherited, generations, precious items from the past, valuable
Bridge............................... Transition, joining of 2 sides
Running............................. Run the race, striving
Sand................................. Weak foundation
Real Estate .... Buy territory, sell territoy
Dresser .... Storage, or if overflowing storage issues
Candle .... Christ, lighting up darkness, light

_____

_____

_____

_____

_____

_____

_____

_____

A Miscellaneous

B Miscellaneous

Book

C Miscellaneous

Calendar _____

_____

_____

_____

_____

_____

_____

_____

_____

_____

_____

_____

_____

_____

_____

_____

_____

_____

D Miscellaneous

E Miscellaneous

F Miscellaneous

G Miscellaneous

H Miscellaneous

I Miscellaneous

J Miscellaneous

K Miscellaneous

L Miscellaneous

M Miscellaneous

N Miscellaneous

O Miscellaneous

P Miscellaneous

Q Miscellaneous

R Miscellaneous

S Miscellaneous

T Miscellaneous

U Miscellaneous

V Miscellaneous

W Miscellaneous

X Miscellaneous

Y Miscellaneous

Z Miscellaneous

Your Title:_____

_____

_____

_____

_____

_____

_____

_____

_____

_____

_____

_____

_____

_____

_____

_____

_____

_____

_____

Your Title:＿＿＿＿＿＿＿

Your Title:_____

_____

_____

_____

_____

_____

_____

_____

_____

_____

_____

_____

_____

_____

_____

_____

_____

_____

_____

_____

Your Title:_____

_____

_____

_____

_____

_____

_____

_____

_____

_____

_____

_____

_____

_____

_____

_____

_____

_____

_____

_____

_____

Your Title: _____

_____

_____

_____

_____

_____

_____

_____

_____

_____

_____

_____

_____

_____

_____

_____

_____

_____

_____

Your Title: _____

_____

_____

_____

_____

_____

_____

_____

_____

_____

_____

_____

_____

_____

_____

_____

_____

_____

_____

_____

Your Title: _____

Part Three:
Dream Journal Pages

Introduction

Welcome to the wonderful, supernatural realm of dreams and dream interpretation. I love it when God speaks to me through dreams, and I know you will too.

Through my own personal experience and helping others with their dreams, God inspired me to create a simple, easy way to record dreams and their interpretation. This journal will serve as a resource for the present, as well as a reference for easy retrieval of past dreams.

Part Three: Dream Journal Pages is designed in such a way that it will be easy to locate a dream when you want to refer back to it. This is your dream journal; use it you choose. However, I've included helpful hints on how it is designed to be used. Ultimately, the most important thing and the number one rule is: Write it down, write it down, write it down!

Be Blessed and Sweet Dreams!

Helpful Hints To Utilize This Journal

1. Keep this journal, a pencil, and a night light by your bed to record your dreams.

2. As soon as you wake, check your memory to see if you recall a dream. Then write it down immediately. Dreams can fly away and never be remembered. (Job 20:8)

3. Always record the date you received a dream. Also, it is important to note if you are on vacation or in a place other than your home.

4. Record your dream on the left-hand side of the journal pages titled "*Dream*." The right-hand side, titled "*Dream Interpretation*," is for you to write out symbol meanings, the interpretation, and the dreams message.

Sample Journal Entry

Dream	Dream Interpretation
Date: 10.9.03 Title: Helicopter Ride with Jesus I was flying a helicopter. I think Jesus was with me; I'm not sure which one of us was flying. We were surveying the land when the helicopter tilted so we could see better and this is what I saw...	Helicopter: angelic realm... seeing from a position in the spirit realm. Interpretation: The Lord is allowing me to see from a position in the spirit realm the lay of the land ... what is before me.

5. I suggest keeping a record of your personal dream symbols in one place by utilizing the "part two" section of this book for easy reference. As you dream, have visions, or see pictures, God will use people, things, and places that have a specific meaning to you. God will develop a special dream language just for you.

6. Title each dream, vision, or picture and assign it a topic. A dream topic would include something such as: personal, work, ministry, family, guidance, warning, prophetic, etc.

7. Using pencil to make your dream interpretation notes is beneficial until you "figure out" the full interpretation, then write it in pen to have a permanent record.

8. Finally, always record your information in the Table of Contents for future, quick reference.

Sample Table of Contents Entry

Date	Title	Topic	Page
10.9.03	Helicopter Ride w/Jesus	Spiritual Growth	1
1.17.04	Stock Market	Personal Growth	7
2.10.04	"X" Marks the spot	Spiritual Growth	9

Please remember: *The Part Three: Dream Journal Pages* are for your personal use. The steps and suggestions listed above are just helpful hints. Use this journal however it will best suit you. It is designed to help you.

As you develop the habit of writing out your dreams, visions, and pictures I know that you will discover the exciting ways God speaks. I pray that God will impart to you His supernatural ability for interpretation especially through the avenue of dreams.

May God grant you wisdom to unlock the secrets He speaks to you, and may you enjoy hearing from your Heavenly Father through this exciting avenue.

Sweet Dreams!

Contents

Date	Title	Topic	Page

Contents

Date	Title	Topic	Page

Contents

Date	Title	Topic	Page

Contents

Date	Title	Topic	Page

Dream Title:_____ Date: _____

_____

_____

_____

_____

_____

_____

_____

_____

_____

_____

_____

_____

_____

_____

_____

_____

_____

_____

_____

_____

_____

Dream Interpretation

_____

_____

_____

_____

_____

_____

_____

_____

_____

_____

_____

_____

_____

_____

_____

_____

_____

_____

_____

Dream Title:_____ Date: _____

_____

_____

_____

_____

_____

_____

_____

_____

_____

_____

_____

_____

_____

_____

_____

_____

_____

_____

_____

_____

Dream Interpretation

_____

_____

_____

_____

_____

_____

_____

_____

_____

_____

_____

_____

_____

_____

_____

_____

_____

_____

_____

Dream Title:_____ Date: _____

_____

_____

_____

_____

_____

_____

_____

_____

_____

_____

_____

_____

_____

_____

_____

_____

_____

_____

Dream Interpretation

Dream Title:_____ Date: _____

_____

_____

_____

_____

_____

_____

_____

_____

_____

_____

_____

_____

_____

_____

_____

_____

_____

_____

_____

Dream Interpretation

Dream Title:_____ Date: _____

_____

_____

_____

_____

_____

_____

_____

_____

_____

_____

_____

_____

_____

_____

_____

_____

_____

_____

Dream Interpretation

Dream Title:_____ Date: _____

_____

_____

_____

_____

_____

_____

_____

_____

_____

_____

_____

_____

_____

_____

_____

_____

_____

_____

_____

Dream Interpretation

_____

_____

_____

_____

_____

_____

_____

_____

_____

_____

_____

_____

_____

_____

_____

_____

_____

_____

_____

_____

Dream Title:_____ Date: _____

_____

_____

_____

_____

_____

_____

_____

_____

_____

_____

_____

_____

_____

_____

_____

_____

_____

_____

Dream Interpretation

Dream Title:_____ Date: _____

_____

_____

_____

_____

_____

_____

_____

_____

_____

_____

_____

_____

_____

_____

_____

_____

_____

_____

_____

_____

Dream Interpretation

Dream Title:_____ Date: _____

_____

_____

_____

_____

_____

_____

_____

_____

_____

_____

_____

_____

_____

_____

_____

_____

_____

_____

_____

_____

Dream Interpretation

Dream Title:_____ Date:_____

_____

_____

_____

_____

_____

_____

_____

_____

_____

_____

_____

_____

_____

_____

_____

_____

_____

_____

_____

_____

Dream Interpretation

Dream Title:_____ Date: _____

_____

_____

_____

_____

_____

_____

_____

_____

_____

_____

_____

_____

_____

_____

_____

_____

_____

_____

_____

Dream Interpretation

_____

_____

_____

_____

_____

_____

_____

_____

_____

_____

_____

_____

_____

_____

_____

_____

_____

_____

Dream Title:_____ Date: _____

_____

_____

_____

_____

_____

_____

_____

_____

_____

_____

_____

_____

_____

_____

_____

_____

_____

_____

_____

_____

_____

_____

Dream Interpretation

Dream Title:_____ Date:_____

_____

_____

_____

_____

_____

_____

_____

_____

_____

_____

_____

_____

_____

_____

_____

_____

_____

_____

_____

Dream Interpretation

_____

_____

_____

_____

_____

_____

_____

_____

_____

_____

_____

_____

_____

_____

_____

_____

_____

_____

_____

Dream Title:_____ Date: _____

_____

_____

_____

_____

_____

_____

_____

_____

_____

_____

_____

_____

_____

_____

_____

_____

_____

_____

_____

_____

_____

Dream Interpretation

_____

_____

_____

_____

_____

_____

_____

_____

_____

_____

_____

_____

_____

_____

_____

_____

_____

_____

_____

_____

_____

Dream Title:_____ Date: _____

_____

_____

_____

_____

_____

_____

_____

_____

_____

_____

_____

_____

_____

_____

_____

_____

_____

_____

_____

Dream Interpretation

Dream Title:_____ Date: _____

_____
_____
_____
_____
_____
_____
_____
_____
_____
_____
_____
_____
_____
_____
_____
_____
_____
_____
_____
_____
_____
_____
_____

Dream Interpretation

_____

_____

_____

_____

_____

_____

_____

_____

_____

_____

_____

_____

_____

_____

_____

_____

_____

_____

Dream Title:_____ Date:_____

_____

_____

_____

_____

_____

_____

_____

_____

_____

_____

_____

_____

_____

_____

_____

_____

_____

_____

_____

_____

Dream Interpretation

Dream Title:_____ Date: _____

_____
_____
_____
_____
_____
_____
_____
_____
_____
_____
_____
_____
_____
_____
_____
_____
_____
_____
_____
_____

Dream Interpretation

Dream Title:_____ Date: _____

_____

_____

_____

_____

_____

_____

_____

_____

_____

_____

_____

_____

_____

_____

_____

_____

_____

_____

_____

_____

Dream Interpretation

Dream Title:_____ Date: _____

_____

_____

_____

_____

_____

_____

_____

_____

_____

_____

_____

_____

_____

_____

_____

_____

_____

_____

Dream Interpretation

_____

_____

_____

_____

_____

_____

_____

_____

_____

_____

_____

_____

_____

_____

_____

_____

_____

_____

_____

Dream Title:_____ Date:_____

_____

_____

_____

_____

_____

_____

_____

_____

_____

_____

_____

_____

_____

_____

_____

_____

_____

_____

_____

Dream Interpretation

_____

_____

_____

_____

_____

_____

_____

_____

_____

_____

_____

_____

_____

_____

_____

_____

_____

Dream Title:_____ Date: _____

_____

_____

_____

_____

_____

_____

_____

_____

_____

_____

_____

_____

_____

_____

_____

_____

_____

Dream Interpretation

Dream Title:_____ Date: _____

_____
_____
_____
_____
_____
_____
_____
_____
_____
_____
_____
_____
_____
_____
_____
_____
_____
_____
_____
_____
_____

Dream Interpretation

_____

_____

_____

_____

_____

_____

_____

_____

_____

_____

_____

_____

_____

_____

_____

_____

_____

_____

_____

_____

Dream Title:_____ Date:_____

_____

_____

_____

_____

_____

_____

_____

_____

_____

_____

_____

_____

_____

_____

_____

_____

_____

_____

_____

_____

_____

Dream Interpretation

_____

_____

_____

_____

_____

_____

_____

_____

_____

_____

_____

_____

_____

_____

_____

_____

_____

_____

Dream Title:_____ Date: _____

_____

_____

_____

_____

_____

_____

_____

_____

_____

_____

_____

_____

_____

_____

_____

_____

_____

_____

_____

_____

Dream Interpretation

Below is a partial list of Scripture references to dreams that are found in the Bible. Please note: The Bible also uses phrases like "visions of my head upon my bed" or "night visions" when referring to dreams.

Bible References to Dreams

Genesis 20:3,6
Genesis 28:12
Genesis 31:10-11
Genesis 31:24
Genesis 37:5-20
Genesis 40:5-16
Genesis 41:1-32
Genesis 42:9
Numbers 12:6
Deuteronomy 13:1-5
Judges 7:13-15
1 Samuel 28:6,15
1 Kings 3:5,15
Job 7:14
Job 20:8
Job 33:15
Psalms 73:20
Psalms 126:1
Ecclesiastes 5:3,7
Isaiah 29:7-8

Jeremiah 23:25-32
Jeremiah 27:9
Jeremiah 29:8
Daniel 1:17
Daniel 2:1-45
Daniel 4:5-19
Daniel 5:12
Daniel 7:1
Joel 2:28
Zechariah 10:2
Matthew 1:20
Matthew 2:12-22
Matthew 27:19
Acts 2:17
Jude 1:8

Debbie Kitterman is a breath of fresh air! With a down-to-earth teaching style, she's both accessible and fun as she unpacks solid Scriptural truths.

As a prophetic encourager, she partners with churches and individuals to realize their spiritual potential. Debbie is passionate about helping people claim their God-given inheritance as partners with Him in the work of the Gospel. Her teachings inspire faith to believe in and expect the impossible.

Debbie is an ordained Foursquare pastor currently serving with her husband as senior pastors of Restoration Church in Lacey, Washington. She is the author of *Releasing God's Heart Through Hearing His Voice* and an international speaker. She is the founder and teacher of D2HTraining.com, an online course designed to equip believers in releasing God's heart. She has been married to her high school sweetheart John for 31 years and they have two grown children.

Other Books and material by Debbie Kitterman can be found on her website here: https://debbiekitterman.com/shop/

Releasing God's Heart through Hearing His Voice Training Manual. Available in English and Spanish.

Becoming Kingdom Kids Releasing God's Heart through Hearing His Voice Training Manual for kids.

The Gift of Prophetic Encouragement: Hearing the Words of God for Others

Online Training: www.d2htraining.com

Send all inquiries or ministry invitations to the email or address below. Or fill out the inquiry form on Debbie's website at: https://debbiekitterman.com/contact-us/

Additional copies of this book, mp3 downloads, other teaching materials, and mentoring/coaching services are available on our web site: https://debbiekitterman.com/

email: info@dare2hear.com

Send a request for product inquires/orders to:

Dare 2 Hear
PO Box 5077
Lacey, WA 98509-5077

Endnotes

1 See page 142 at the back of this book for references to dreams

2 1 John 4:1

3 Dreammoods.com

4 Kitterman, Debbie. Releasing God's Heart through Hearing His Voice. Olympia: Dare 2 Hear/Sound the Call Publications © 2008, 2011. Page 132

5 Dictionary.com

6 Dictionary.com

7 Genesis 20

8 Matthew 2

9 Genesis 40

10 Genesis 41

11 Genesis 37:5

12 Kitterman, Debbie. Releasing God's Heart through Hearing His Voice. Olympia: Dare 2 Hear/Sound the Call Publications © 2008, 2011. Page 135

13 Job 33:14-16 NKJV

14 Genesis 20:3

15 Genesis 31:24

16 Genesis 40:5

17 Genesis 41:1,5

18 Judges 7:13-14

19 Daniel 2

20 Matthew 2:12

21 Matthew 27:19

22 Daniel 5:11-26

23 Job 20:8 ESV

24 For a fuller teaching on dreams including the many purposes of dreams you can purchase a copy of Releasing God's Heart through Hearing His Voice pages 137-145 or check out the individual training classes at www.d2htraining.com

25 Psalm 119:105

26 This is not an exhaustive list. There are many other types of dreams throughout Scripture. Feel free to add to the list.

27 Dictionary.com

Made in USA - Kendallville, IN
1208113_9780984012343
12.08.2020 0823